Franklin's
TREES

A.J. SCHENKMAN

Illustrated by **Lauren Reese**

muddy boots™

Essex, Connecticut

Franklin Delano Roosevelt grew up on his parent's estate in Hyde Park, New York. He was born on January 30, 1882.

Franklin was surrounded by trees at an early age.

He loved trees and spending time outdoors.

Franklin planted trees with his father, James. He liked pine trees, oak trees, maple trees, and, one of his favorites, the tulip poplar. Throughout Franklin's life, as a child and as president of the United States, it is believed that he oversaw the planting of more than a million trees.

Franklin was surrounded by nature. He noticed
all the wonderful birds who called his trees home.
Franklin spent hours every day learning all he could
about the birds and which trees they liked.

Goldfinch and Maple

Bluebird and Dogwood

Cardinal and spruce

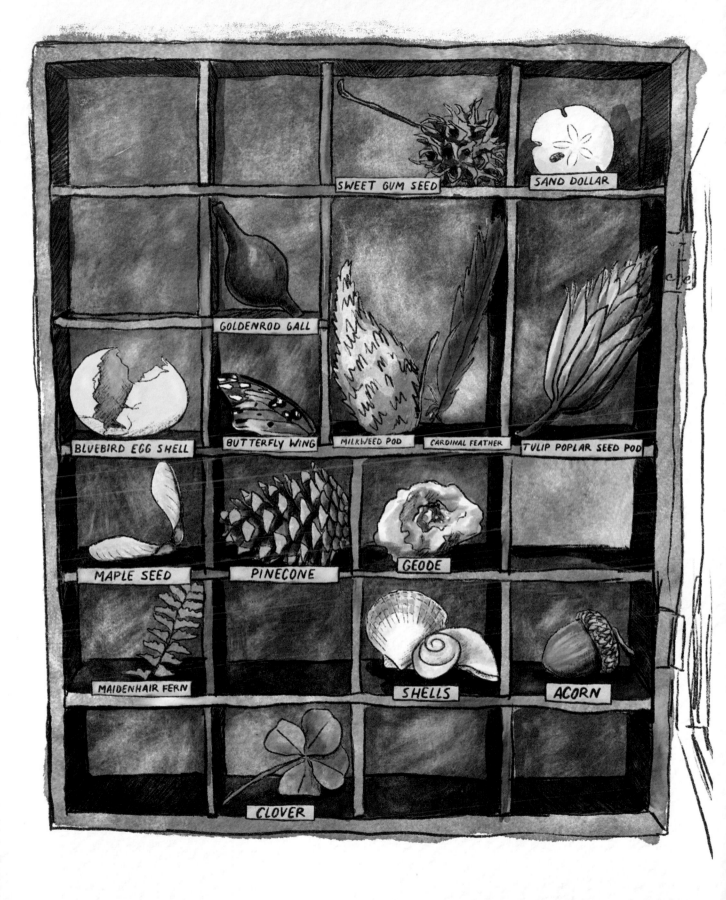

When he was older, Franklin met Eleanor. They married in 1905. The two of them frequently liked to picnic under the trees around the estate. He told Eleanor that he found trees relaxing. He enjoyed their shade and beauty.

Later, he shared that love of trees with his children.

Even though FDR, as people called him, became a state senator, governor of New York, and, later, president of the United States, he referred to himself as a simple tree farmer.

Every chance he had, FDR visited his home in Hyde Park.
It was where he felt most comfortable.

"All that is within me cries out to go back to my home on the Hudson River," Franklin once said.

Whenever the family could not locate FDR, Eleanor knew that her husband was walking the trails looking at all the trees he had planted. If he was not walking, he was riding his favorite horse, Bobby, on the trails.

In 1921, Franklin came down with polio. He lost the use of his legs. Franklin became sad because he could no longer visit his trees. He could only look at them from his bedroom window.

Franklin wanted to walk again.

He hoped to stand tall like the mighty oaks and maples
that lined the driveway leading to his home.
Franklin drew strength from the tree-lined drive.

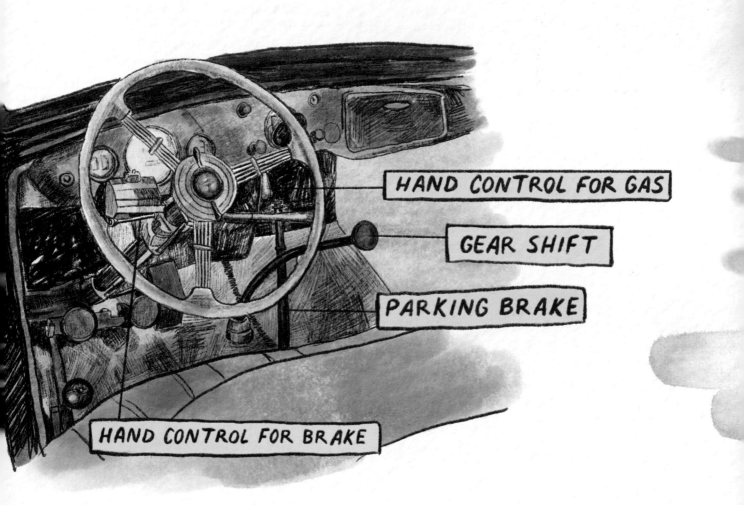

HAND CONTROL FOR GAS

GEAR SHIFT

PARKING BRAKE

HAND CONTROL FOR BRAKE

Franklin never regained the use of his legs, but he had
a car built that he could operate with his hands.

Once again, Franklin was able to visit his trees. He
widened the trails into roads so he could look over his trees.

When FDR became president in 1933, the country was in bad shape. The Great Depression had started in 1929 and many people were out of work. FDR put people to work with lots of programs paid for by the US government.

One program was the Civilian Conservation Corps or CCC.
The CCC became known as "Roosevelt's Tree Army" because
they planted millions of trees all over the United States.

During the Great Depression there was also a great
drought that caused the Dust Bowl. When farmers planted,
they had cleared all the vegetation. There was no rain for a long
time, so the land dried up. When the wind blew, it picked up the
precious topsoil and created huge dust storms.

Once again, trees were the answer.
Roosevelt's Tree Army went to work.

Another big event when Franklin was president was
World War II. His trees helped win the war.

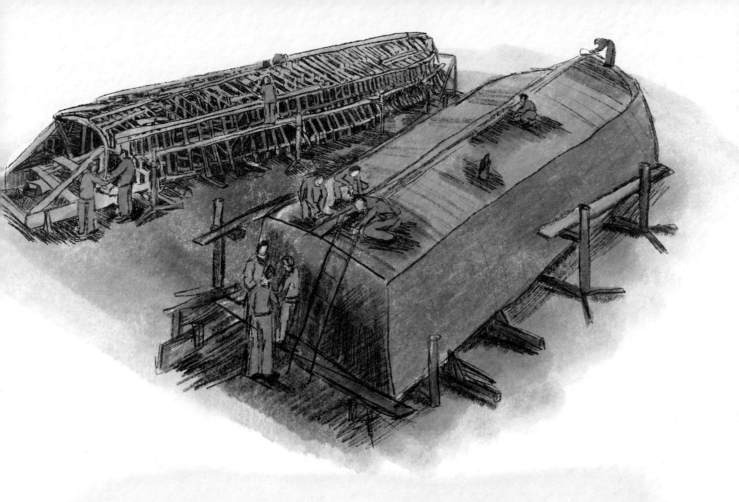

Oak trees, known for their strength,
were used to build patrol boats for the US Navy.

Franklin loved Christmas. He especially loved the Norway spruces used for Christmas trees. All year, they reminded him of one of his favorite holidays. Their smell cheered him up and reminded him of the woods of Hyde Park.

In order to lift the spirits of Winston Churchill, England's wartime prime minister, FDR sent his friend one of his best Christmas trees.

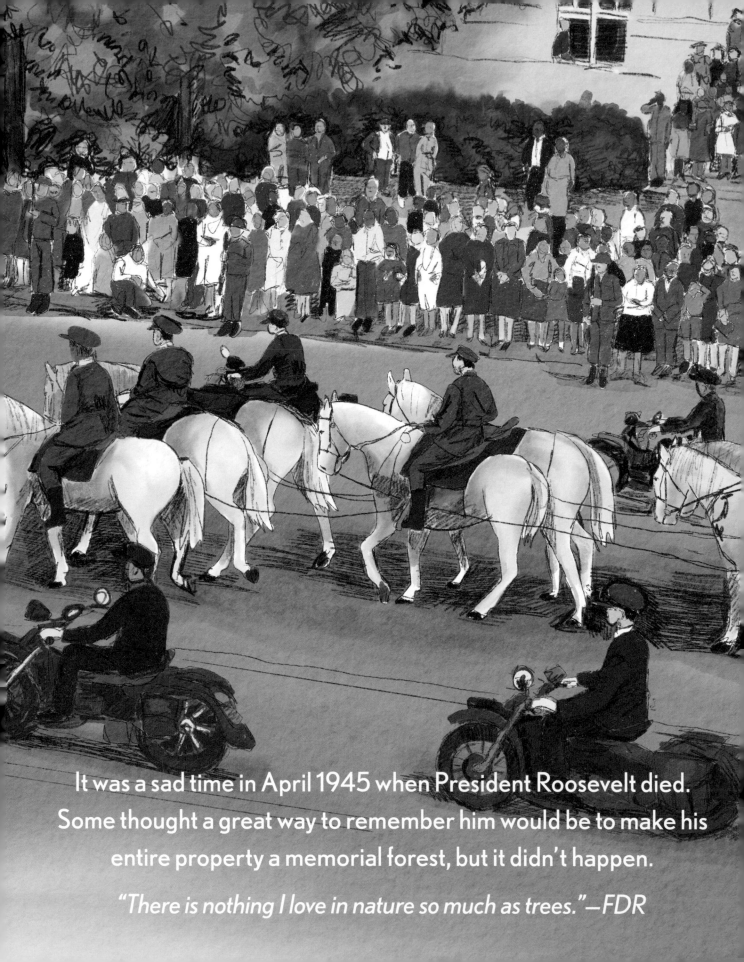

It was a sad time in April 1945 when President Roosevelt died. Some thought a great way to remember him would be to make his entire property a memorial forest, but it didn't happen.

"There is nothing I love in nature so much as trees." —FDR

Franklin was buried in his mother's rose garden in view of the old oaks, maples, pine, and tulip poplar trees he had known as a child.

Today many people visit FDR's house and property. It is a historic site owned by the US government. On any given day, families walk the same trails and roads that FDR did. People also sit under some of the same trees that gave him so much joy.

TREE IDENTIFICATION

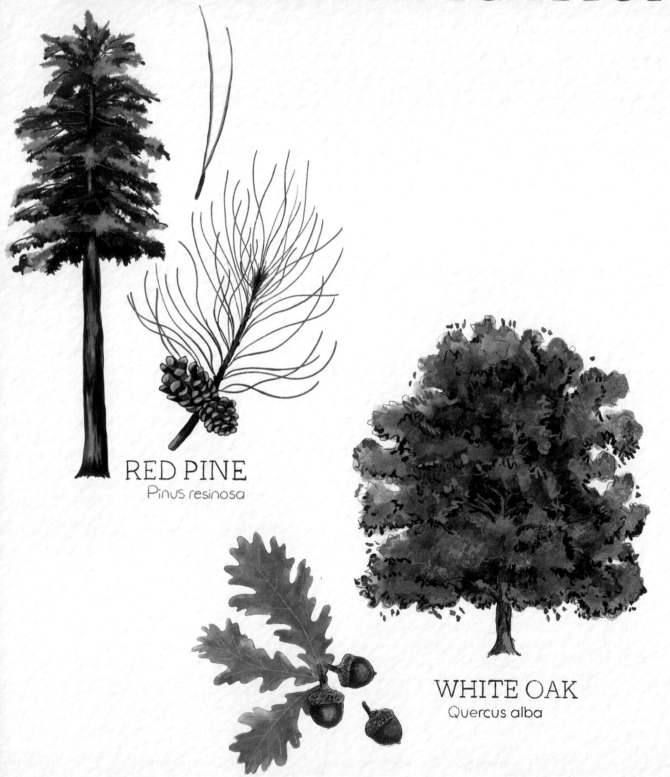

RED PINE
Pinus resinosa

WHITE OAK
Quercus alba

RED MAPLE
Acer rubrum

TULIP POPLAR
Liriodendron tulipifera

To Aunt Linda

we jump in puddles

An imprint of Globe Pequot, the trade division of
The Rowman & Littlefield Publishing Group, Inc.
4501 Forbes Blvd., Ste. 200
Lanham, MD 20706
www.rowman.com

www.MuddyBootsBooks.com

Distributed by NATIONAL BOOK NETWORK

Text copyright © 2024 by Adam J. Schenkman

Illustrations copyright © 2024 by Lauren Reese

British Library Cataloguing in
Publication Information Available

Library of Congress
Cataloging-in-Publication Data Available

ISBN 978-1-4930-7737-3 (cloth)
ISBN 978-1-4930-8581-1 (ebook)

Printed in New Delhi, India
February 2024